BENEDICT BENED

salzburg Travel Guide

Exploring Salzburg, Austria: Unlock the Melodies of Mozart's Hometown, Insider Tips, Must-Visit Gems, and Money-Saving Strategies for the Savvy Traveler!

Dedication:

To the enchanting city of Salzburg,

This travel guide is dedicated to the captivating spirit and timeless allure of Salzburg. It is a heartfelt tribute to the melodic symphony that dances through its streets, the rich tapestry of history that weaves through its ancient landmarks, and the warm embrace of its people.

Contents

Preface

Welcome to "Exploring Salzburg, Austria: Unlock the Melodies of Mozart's Hometown"! Get ready to embark on an extraordinary journey through the enchanting city of Salzburg, where history, music, and natural beauty harmoniously blend together to create a truly captivating experience. This travel guide is your key to unlocking the hidden treasures, must-visit landmarks, insider tips, and money-saving strategies that will make your Salzburg adventure extraordinary.

Picture yourself strolling through the picturesque streets of Salzburg, where every corner holds a story and every building exudes a sense of timeless elegance. Known worldwide as the birthplace of the prodigious composer Wolfgang Amadeus Mozart, Salzburg is steeped in musical heritage, its very air infused with the melodies that have enchanted generations. As you wander through the city, it's as if the notes of Mozart's symphonies follow your every step, creating a harmonious backdrop to your explorations.

Salzburg's historic center, a UNESCO World Heritage site, transports you to a bygone era. The resplendent architecture, meticulously preserved over centuries, showcases the city's rich past. From the majestic Mirabell Palace and its stunning gardens to the iconic Hohensalzburg Fortress perched atop the

Festungsberg hill, the cityscape unfolds like a living canvas, inviting you to immerse yourself in its grandeur.

But Salzburg is not just a city frozen in time; it thrives with a dynamic energy that resonates through its vibrant streets. As you delve deeper, you'll discover a modern city that seamlessly blends tradition with innovation. From the bustling markets brimming with local flavors and handicrafts to the contemporary art galleries and avant-garde performances, Salzburg offers a sensory feast for the discerning traveler.

As your knowledgeable guide, I will lead you through the myriad of experiences that Salzburg has to offer. Together, we'll navigate the maze-like streets, uncover hidden gems, and reveal the insider secrets that will make your visit truly exceptional. Whether you're a history buff, a music aficionado, a food lover, or simply an adventurer seeking new horizons, Salzburg has something to captivate your imagination.

Throughout this guide, you'll find practical tips to make the most of your time in Salzburg. From planning your journey and choosing the perfect accommodations to navigating the city's transportation system and uncovering money-saving strategies, every aspect of your trip is carefully considered. You'll also find comprehensive information on must-visit landmarks, including detailed descriptions, historical insights, and insider recommendations to ensure you don't miss a single highlight.

But this guide is more than just a compilation of facts and figures. It's a narrative that weaves together the threads of history, culture, and local life, inviting you to become an active participant in the vibrant tapestry of Salzburg. Through interactive maps, engaging anecdotes, and immersive descriptions, you'll be transported to the heart of the city, enabling you to experience Salzburg as if you were a seasoned local.

So, join me on this extraordinary adventure as we unravel the melodies of Mozart's hometown, explore the hidden corners of Salzburg's rich heritage, and embrace the charm that has captivated travelers for centuries. Together, let's create memories that will resonate with you long after you've bid farewell to this enchanting city. Are you ready to unlock the secrets of Salzburg? Let the journey begin!

I

Part One

Essential Travel Information

Chapter 1

Discovering Salzburg : A Captivating Prelude

Unveiling the Charms of Salzburg

Welcome to the captivating city of Salzburg, where history, music, and natural beauty intertwine to create an irresistible destination. In this chapter, we invite you to delve into the enchanting charms that await you in every corner of Salzburg.

As you step foot in Salzburg, you'll find yourself immersed in a city that exudes a timeless elegance. The UNESCO World Heritage-listed historic center, with its narrow cobblestone streets and meticulously preserved architecture, transports you back in time. Marvel at the ornate facades, intricately adorned churches, and charming squares that tell tales of Salzburg's rich past.

A walk through the Mirabell Palace and its enchanting gardens is like entering a fairytale. Be captivated by the symphony of colors as flowers bloom and fountains dance in perfect harmony.

This splendid palace, with its Baroque grandeur, is a testament to the city's opulent heritage.

Venture further, and you'll discover the imposing Hohensalzburg Fortress, perched atop the Festungsberg hill. This mighty fortress, one of the largest fully preserved medieval castles in Europe, offers panoramic views that will leave you breathless. Explore its labyrinthine corridors, admire the ancient artifacts, and imagine the stories that echo within its walls.

Salzburg's musical legacy is renowned worldwide, and no visit would be complete without delving into its melodious heritage. The city proudly honors its most famous son, Wolfgang Amadeus Mozart. Visit Mozart's Birthplace, a place of pilgrimage for music enthusiasts, and gain insight into the life and genius of this prodigious composer. As you wander through the rooms where Mozart grew up, you can almost hear the echoes of his melodies lingering in the air.

But Salzburg's charms extend beyond Mozart. Allow yourself to be swept away by the melodies of "The Sound of Music" as you visit iconic filming locations throughout the city. Walk in the footsteps of Maria and the Von Trapp family, and relive the magic of this beloved musical against the backdrop of Salzburg's picturesque landscapes.

As you explore Salzburg, you'll find hidden treasures tucked away in its winding alleyways. Uncover delightful cafes, boutique shops, and charming courtyards that invite you to pause and immerse yourself in the local atmosphere. Engage with the warm and welcoming locals, who will eagerly share stories of their beloved city and offer insider tips on the best-kept secrets of Salzburg.

Salzburg is a city that seamlessly blends tradition with modernity. Alongside its historical landmarks, you'll find contemporary art galleries, innovative museums, and a thriving cultural scene that pulses with creativity. Whether you're an art enthusiast, a lover of classical music, or a theater aficionado, Salzburg offers a vibrant tapestry of cultural experiences to suit every taste.

As you turn the pages of this guide, we will accompany you on an immersive journey through Salzburg, unraveling its charms and guiding you to its hidden gems. From historical landmarks to cultural delights, from culinary adventures to natural beauty, Salzburg will captivate you at every turn.

So, prepare to be enchanted by the charms of Salzburg, as we invite you to explore this captivating city that has inspired countless artists, musicians, and travelers throughout the ages. Let the symphony of Salzburg's charms sweep you off your feet as you embark on an unforgettable adventure. Are you ready to unveil the captivating allure of Salzburg? Let the exploration begin!

A Brief Historical Overture

To truly appreciate the charm and significance of Salzburg, it is essential to delve into its rich historical tapestry. In this chapter, we will take you on a journey through the key epochs and milestones that have shaped the city's captivating history.

Salzburg's story begins over 2,000 years ago, when the Celts first settled in the area. However, it was during the Roman era that the city began to emerge as an important trading hub and strategic outpost. The Romans recognized the natural advantages of Salzburg's location, nestled between the Alps and the Danube River, and established a vibrant community known as "Juvavum." Remnants of this ancient Roman settlement can still be seen today, offering a glimpse into Salzburg's early foundations.

In the 8th century, the city's fate took a decisive turn with the arrival of Saint Rupert. This bishop and missionary played a pivotal role in shaping Salzburg's religious and cultural identity. He established a monastery and laid the foundations for Salzburg's emergence as an ecclesiastical center. Over the centuries, the powerful Prince-Archbishops of Salzburg would wield immense influence, both politically and culturally, leaving an indelible mark on the city's landscape.

During the Middle Ages, Salzburg flourished as a hub of artistic and intellectual activity. Magnificent churches, monasteries, and palaces were constructed, showcasing architectural styles ranging from Romanesque to Gothic. The city became a center for music and patronage, with renowned composers and

6

musicians finding inspiration within its walls.

However, Salzburg's fortunes faced numerous challenges in subsequent centuries. Wars, political turmoil, and the ravages of time took their toll on the city. It was in the late 18th century that Salzburg experienced a renaissance of sorts, thanks to the prodigious talent of Wolfgang Amadeus Mozart. Born in 1756, Mozart's genius brought international acclaim to Salzburg, cementing its status as a musical mecca.

In the 19th and early 20th centuries, Salzburg underwent significant transformations. The city embraced modernization, while still cherishing its historical heritage. The arrival of the railroad in the mid-19th century opened up new opportunities for trade and tourism, connecting Salzburg to the wider world.

Tragically, like many cities, Salzburg was not immune to the turmoil of World War II. The city suffered considerable damage during the conflict, but efforts were made to restore and preserve its architectural treasures in the post-war years. Today, Salzburg stands as a testament to the resilience and determination of its people, who have preserved and cherished their city's cultural legacy.

As you explore Salzburg's streets and squares, you'll encounter a captivating blend of architectural styles. Romanesque, Gothic, Renaissance, Baroque, and Rococo influences can be found side by side, forming a harmonious ensemble that tells the story of the city's past. From the iconic Salzburg Cathedral to the grandeur of Mirabell Palace, each building reflects a different chapter in Salzburg's history.

In this guide, we will unravel the historical threads that have shaped Salzburg, providing you with a deeper understanding of the city's cultural significance. We will guide you through the architectural wonders, regale you with tales of influential figures, and invite you to step back in time as you discover the layers of history that lie beneath Salzburg's charming facade.

So, prepare to be transported through the ages as we embark on a historical journey through Salzburg. From ancient Roman beginnings to the cultural renaissance of Mozart and beyond, we invite you to immerse yourself in the captivating narrative of this extraordinary city. Let the historical overture unfold as you embrace the timeless allure of Salzburg's past.

Embracing the Musical Heritage

Salzburg's soul beats to the rhythm of music, and its streets are alive with the echoes of its rich musical heritage. In this chapter, we invite you to immerse yourself in the melodies and stories that have made Salzburg a renowned center of musical excellence.

Salzburg's most illustrious musical son, Wolfgang Amadeus Mozart, needs no introduction. Born in 1756, Mozart's prodigious talent and creative genius continue to captivate audiences worldwide. The city of Salzburg holds Mozart dear to its heart, and his legacy is celebrated in numerous ways throughout its streets.

A visit to Mozart's Birthplace is a pilgrimage for any music enthusiast. Step into the house where the young Mozart grew up and explore the rooms that witnessed his musical development. From his childhood violin to original scores and personal artifacts, you'll gain a deeper understanding of the man behind the music.

The Mozarteum, a prestigious music conservatory founded in 1841, pays tribute to Mozart's enduring influence on Salzburg's cultural landscape. It offers a platform for young musicians to hone their skills and carry on the city's musical traditions. Attending a performance or concert at the Mozarteum is an opportunity to witness the next generation of talent as they bring Mozart's compositions to life.

No discussion of Salzburg's musical heritage would be complete without mentioning the world-famous Salzburg Festival. Founded in 1920, this annual extravaganza of opera, theater, and classical music draws artists and spectators from all corners of the globe. The festival takes place in various venues across the city, including the stunning Salzburg Festival Hall and the grandiose Felsenreitschule, a former riding school turned open-air theater. Immerse yourself in the magical ambiance of the festival and revel in the transcendent performances that grace its stages.

Beyond Mozart, Salzburg boasts a vibrant music scene that embraces a range of genres and styles. The Salzburg Cathedral, with its awe-inspiring Baroque architecture, hosts regular organ concerts that showcase the majestic sound of this iconic instrument. Jazz lovers can find their rhythm at cozy clubs that feature live performances by talented local and international artists.

Salzburg's commitment to preserving its musical heritage is evident in its numerous music museums and exhibitions. The Museum of Mozart's Instruments offers a fascinating insight into the instruments Mozart himself played, while the Salzburg Museum showcases the city's broader musical history. Interactive exhibits, multimedia presentations, and rare artifacts transport you back in time, allowing you to experience the magic of Salzburg's musical legacy firsthand.

As you explore Salzburg's streets, you may even stumble upon impromptu performances by street musicians, further enhancing the city's enchanting atmosphere. These serenades in unexpected corners create unforgettable moments of harmony between artist and audience.

In this guide, we will guide you to the very heart of Salzburg's musical heritage. From Mozart's footsteps to the modern notes that reverberate throughout the city, we will lead you on a melodic journey of discovery. We'll provide insights into the city's music scene, offer recommendations for exceptional performances, and uncover hidden gems that celebrate Salzburg's musical traditions.

So, let the melodies guide you as you embrace the musical heritage of Salzburg. Immerse yourself in the harmonies that have enchanted the world for centuries, and experience firsthand why Salzburg is truly a city of music. From classical masterpieces to contemporary rhythms, Salzburg invites you to be part of its symphony. Let the music resonate within you as you explore the rich musical tapestry that weaves through the city's streets.

Chapter 2

Planning Your Journey: Practical Tips and Resources

When to Go: Seasons and Festivals

W hen planning your visit to Salzburg, it's important to consider the seasons and the vibrant festivals that bring the city to life. Each time of year offers a unique experience, whether you're captivated by the winter wonderland or enchanted by the warm summer days. In this chapter, we will guide you through the seasons and highlight the festivals that make Salzburg a year-round destination.

Salzburg experiences four distinct seasons, each with its own charm and allure. Let's explore the characteristics of each season to help you decide when to embark on your Salzburg adventure.

- **Spring:** From March to May, Salzburg emerges from its winter slumber as nature awakens. The city is adorned with blooming flowers, and the surrounding countryside transforms into a lush green landscape. Spring in Salzburg is a time of renewal, perfect for exploring the city's gardens, taking leisurely walks along the Salzach River, and enjoying outdoor cafes as the weather becomes milder.

- **Summer:** June to August brings warm and pleasant weather, making it an ideal time to explore the city's outdoor attractions. The streets come alive with locals and tourists alike, soaking up the sun and immersing themselves in the lively atmosphere. Summer is also festival season in Salzburg, with the renowned Salzburg Festival taking center stage. This world-class event attracts top performers from around the globe and offers a range of opera, theater, and classical music performances.

- **Autumn:** September to November paints Salzburg in vibrant hues of red, orange, and gold as the foliage changes. The city takes on a peaceful and romantic ambiance, making it an ideal time for leisurely walks through the parks and gardens. Autumn in Salzburg also brings the magical Salzburg Culture Days, a celebration of local arts and culture featuring exhibitions, concerts, and theatrical performances.

- **Winter:** December to February blankets Salzburg in a layer of enchantment as snowflakes delicately fall, transforming the city into a winter wonderland. The holiday season is particularly magical, with festive markets adorning the squares and streets. The melodies of Christmas fill the air, and the smell of freshly baked gingerbread and mulled wine entices visitors. Winter in Salzburg offers the opportunity to enjoy skiing in the nearby Alps or cozy up in historic cafes, savoring warm drinks and indulgent pastries.

Alongside the seasons, Salzburg's festivals add a captivating element to the city's cultural calendar. In addition to the Salzburg Festival, other notable events include the Easter Festival, featuring world-class orchestras and renowned conductors, and the Mozart Week, celebrating the musical genius of Mozart with a series of concerts and performances.

When planning your visit, it's important to consider that peak tourist seasons in Salzburg are during the summer months and around the major festivals. It's advisable to book accommodations and tickets in advance during these periods to ensure availability.

In this guide, we will provide you with essential information on the best times to visit Salzburg based on your preferences, including the climate, festival schedules, and crowd levels. Whether you long for the lively atmosphere of summer or the cozy charm of winter, we'll help you plan your journey to make the most of your time in Salzburg.

So, consider the seasons and festivals that resonate with you as you plan your visit to Salzburg. Each time of year has its own enchanting qualities, ensuring that your experience in this musical city will be truly unforgettable. Prepare to be immersed in the vibrant atmosphere and rich cultural tapestry of Salzburg, no matter which season you choose to explore.

Navigating Salzburg: Transportation and Getting Around

Once you've decided on the perfect time to visit Salzburg, it's important to familiarize yourself with the various transportation options available in the city. In this chapter, we'll guide you through the efficient and convenient ways to navigate Salzburg, ensuring a smooth and enjoyable journey.

1. Public Transportation:

Salzburg boasts a well-developed public transportation system that makes getting around the city a breeze. The buses, trams, and S-Bahn trains offer reliable and efficient services, connecting major attractions, neighborhoods, and suburbs. The Salzburg Verkehrsverbund (SVV) oversees the public transportation network, and you can easily purchase tickets from vending machines at bus and tram stops or online. Day passes and multi-day tickets are available for unlimited travel within a specified time frame, offering excellent value for money.

2. Walking:

Salzburg's compact size and pedestrian-friendly layout make it an ideal city for exploring on foot. The historic center, with its narrow streets and charming squares, is best experienced by strolling through its enchanting alleys. As you walk, you'll encounter hidden gems, picturesque courtyards, and architectural marvels at every turn. Walking not only allows you to fully immerse yourself in the city's atmosphere but also gives you the freedom to discover its hidden corners and serendipitous delights.

3. Bicycles:

For the eco-conscious traveler or those seeking an active adventure, cycling is a fantastic way to explore Salzburg. The city offers an extensive network of cycling paths that weave through parks, along the Salzach River, and connect key attractions. You can rent bicycles from various rental shops or use the StadtRAD Salzburg bike-sharing system for short journeys. Exploring Salzburg on two wheels provides a unique perspective, allowing you to cover more ground while enjoying the scenic beauty of the city.

4. Taxis and Rideshares:

Taxis are readily available throughout Salzburg, providing a convenient option for reaching specific destinations or traveling with heavy luggage. You can find taxi stands at prominent locations, or simply hail a cab on the street. Additionally, rideshare services like Uber operate in Salzburg, offering an alternative to traditional taxis. Using a rideshare app allows you to book a car and conveniently reach your desired destination with ease.

5. Salzburg Card:

Consider purchasing the Salzburg Card, a valuable option for travelers looking to make the most of their time in the city. This all-inclusive card provides free admission to major attractions, unlimited use of public transportation, and discounts on various tours and services. It's available for 24, 48, or 72 hours, allowing you to explore Salzburg at your own pace while enjoying significant cost savings.

Whether you choose to hop on a tram, wander through the

streets on foot, or pedal your way around the city, Salzburg's transportation options will ensure a seamless and enjoyable journey. Get ready to navigate Salzburg with confidence, allowing you to focus on the sights, sounds, and experiences that await you in this magnificent city.

Where to Stay: Accommodation Options for Every Budget

Choosing the right accommodation is a key aspect of planning your trip to Salzburg. The city offers a range of options to suit every budget and preference, from luxurious hotels to cozy guesthouses and budget-friendly hostels. In this chapter, we'll guide you through the different areas to stay in Salzburg and provide recommendations for accommodation that will make your stay comfortable and memorable.

1. Historic Center (Altstadt):

For a truly immersive experience, staying in Salzburg's historic center is the perfect choice. The Altstadt is a UNESCO World Heritage site, and it's where you'll find charming cobblestone streets, grand squares, and iconic landmarks. From luxury hotels housed in historic buildings to boutique guesthouses and traditional pensions, there are accommodation options to suit a range of budgets. Staying in the Altstadt allows you to be within walking distance of Salzburg's major attractions, including Mozart's Birthplace, Salzburg Cathedral, and Mirabell Palace.

2. Nonntal:

Located just south of the Altstadt, the Nonntal neighborhood offers a quieter and more residential ambiance while still being within easy reach of the city center. Here, you'll find a mix of hotels, guesthouses, and apartments, providing a tranquil retreat away from the bustling tourist areas. Nonntal is known for its picturesque streets and its proximity to the Hohensalzburg Fortress, which provides stunning views over the city.

3. Linzergasse:

Linzergasse is a vibrant neighborhood located just outside the Altstadt. This lively area is home to a variety of shops, cafes, and restaurants, making it a great choice for those who want to be close to the action while enjoying a local atmosphere. Accommodation options in Linzergasse range from charming bed and breakfasts to mid-range hotels, offering comfort and convenience for travelers.

4. Mirabell District:

On the opposite side of the Salzach River from the Altstadt lies the Mirabell district. This area is known for its beautiful Mirabell Gardens and the famous Mirabell Palace. It offers a mix of accommodation options, including upscale hotels and budget-friendly guesthouses. Staying in the Mirabell district allows you to enjoy a quieter environment while still being within walking distance of the main attractions.

5. New Town (Neustadt):

If you prefer a more modern and cosmopolitan atmosphere, the New Town, or Neustadt, is an excellent choice. This area is characterized by its wide boulevards, shopping streets, and a variety of dining options. Hotels in the New Town range from upscale establishments to budget-friendly chains, providing a range of options for different budgets.

It's important to consider factors such as location, proximity to public transportation, and your specific budget when choosing accommodation. Salzburg offers a wide range of options to suit different preferences, ensuring that you'll find a comfortable and convenient place to call home during your visit.

So, let us assist you in finding the ideal accommodation in Salzburg, ensuring a pleasant and restful stay that complements your travel experience. Whether you prefer the historic charm of the Altstadt or the modern vibe of the New Town, Salzburg has a place for every traveler to lay their head and create unforgettable memories.

Savvy Traveler's Checklist: Essential Items and Documents

As a savvy traveler, being well-prepared is essential for a smooth and enjoyable trip to Salzburg. In this chapter, we'll provide you with a comprehensive checklist of essential items and documents to ensure you have everything you need for your journey.

1. Passport and Travel Documents:
Ensure that your passport is valid for the duration of your stay in Salzburg. Check the entry requirements for your country of residence and make sure you have any necessary visas or

permits. Keep a copy of your passport, travel insurance details, and emergency contact information in a separate and secure location.

2. Local Currency and Payment Methods:

Obtain some local currency, the Euro (€), before your arrival in Salzburg. Familiarize yourself with the exchange rates and consider informing your bank about your travel plans to avoid any issues with your debit or credit cards. Additionally, have a mix of payment methods available, such as cash, credit cards, and a travel card, for convenience and flexibility.

3. Travel Insurance:

Protect yourself and your belongings by obtaining comprehensive travel insurance that covers medical expenses, trip cancellation or interruption, and loss or theft of personal belongings. Keep a copy of your insurance policy and emergency contact information easily accessible.

4. Weather-Appropriate Clothing:

Check the weather forecast for Salzburg during your visit and pack clothing suitable for the season. Salzburg experiences a continental climate, so pack layers for variable weather conditions. Don't forget essentials like comfortable walking shoes, a waterproof jacket or umbrella, and any specialized gear if you plan on engaging in outdoor activities.

5. Travel Adapters and Electronics:

Salzburg operates on 230V electricity with Type C and Type F power outlets. Ensure you have the appropriate travel adapters to charge your electronic devices. Don't forget to pack your camera, chargers, extra batteries, and any other electronic devices you may need during your trip.

6. Language and Communication:
While English is commonly spoken in Salzburg, it's helpful to have some basic knowledge of German phrases and greetings. Consider carrying a pocket-sized language guide or a translation app on your smartphone for convenience in communication.

7. Medications and Health Essentials:
If you require prescription medications, ensure you have an adequate supply for the duration of your trip. Pack any necessary over-the-counter medications, a first aid kit, and personal hygiene products. Check if any vaccinations or preventive measures are recommended for your visit to Salzburg and consult your healthcare provider if needed.

8. Maps and Guidebooks:
Carry a map of Salzburg, either in print or as a digital version on your smartphone or tablet. Guidebooks specific to Salzburg can provide valuable insights and recommendations for attractions, dining, and local customs.

9. Travel Locks and Security Measures:
Secure your luggage with sturdy locks to protect your belongings during your journey. Consider using additional security measures such as money belts or travel pouches for keeping your valuables safe while exploring the city.

10. Emergency Contacts and Important Information:
Make a note of important contact numbers, including local

emergency services, your accommodation details, and the nearest embassy or consulate. Having this information readily available can be invaluable in case of an emergency or if you need assistance during your trip.

Remember to review the checklist and adapt it to your personal needs and preferences. Being a savvy traveler means being well-prepared, allowing you to fully enjoy your time in Salzburg with peace of mind.

So, use this checklist as a guide to ensure you have all the necessary items and documents for a seamless and stress-free travel experience in Salzburg. With everything in order, you'll be ready to embark on an unforgettable adventure in this charming city.

Chapter 3

Unraveling Salzburg: Must-See Landmarks and Hidden Gems

Historic Center: Exploring the Heart of Salzburg

Welcome to the captivating historic center of Salzburg, a UNESCO World Heritage site and the beating heart of the city. In this chapter, we will take you on a journey through the enchanting streets and reveal the must-see landmarks and hidden gems that make the historic center a treasure trove of history, culture, and architectural wonders.

1. Salzburg Cathedral (Dom):
A masterpiece of Baroque architecture, Salzburg Cathedral is a must-visit landmark. Step inside to admire the stunning interior, with its ornate chapels, intricate details, and awe-inspiring organ. Don't miss the chance to climb the cathedral's towers for panoramic views of the city and the surrounding Alps.

2. Hohensalzburg Fortress:

Perched atop Festungsberg hill, Hohensalzburg Fortress is one of Europe's largest and best-preserved medieval fortresses. Take a funicular ride or hike up to explore this imposing structure, which offers breathtaking views of Salzburg and houses a museum showcasing the city's history. Don't forget to wander through the fortress's courtyards and visit the Marionette Museum for a unique cultural experience.

3. Mirabell Palace and Gardens:

Experience the elegance of Mirabell Palace and Gardens, a harmonious blend of architecture and nature. Stroll through the meticulously manicured gardens, adorned with fountains, statues, and vibrant flowerbeds. The palace itself is a splendid example of Italian Baroque design and is famous for its stunning Marble Hall, where concerts and weddings take place.

4. Getreidegasse:

Immerse yourself in the charm of Salzburg's most famous shopping street, Getreidegasse. Lined with colorful townhouses adorned with wrought-iron signs, this bustling pedestrian street is a delight to explore. Browse the shops offering traditional crafts, fashion, and local delicacies, and don't miss the opportunity to visit Mozart's Birthplace, a yellow house where the musical prodigy was born.

5. Mozart's Residence:

Delve into the life and legacy of Wolfgang Amadeus Mozart at Mozart's Residence. Located on Makartplatz, this former home of the Mozart family showcases original instruments, memorabilia, and fascinating exhibits that provide insights into the renowned composer's life and works.

6. Salzburg Museum:

Discover the history and culture of Salzburg at the Salzburg Museum. Housed in the Neue Residenz building, the museum offers a comprehensive collection that spans from prehistoric times to the present day. Explore the exhibitions to gain a deeper understanding of Salzburg's rich heritage and its contributions to art, music, and architecture.

7. St. Peter's Abbey and Cemetery:

Step into the tranquil oasis of St. Peter's Abbey, one of the oldest monastic foundations in the German-speaking world. Explore the magnificent St. Peter's Church, known for its exquisite stucco work and frescoes. Adjacent to the abbey is St. Peter's Cemetery, a serene final resting place with ornate tombstones and a peaceful atmosphere.

8. Salzburg Residenz:

Uncover the grandeur of the Salzburg Residenz, the former palace of the ruling Prince-Archbishops. Marvel at the opulent rooms adorned with exquisite furniture, paintings, and tapestries. Visit the Residenz Gallery, which houses an impressive collection of European paintings from the 16th to the 19th centuries.

Beyond these iconic landmarks, the historic center of Salzburg offers a plethora of hidden gems waiting to be discovered. Venture into the narrow side streets to find charming courtyards, architectural gems, and quaint cafes. Explore the vibrant Marktplatz, where a bustling market takes place, offering fresh produce, local products, and culinary delights.

In this guide, we will provide detailed information on each landmark, including its history, significance, and practical tips for visiting. We will also unveil lesser-known attractions and hidden gems that showcase the unique character of Salzburg's historic center.

Prepare to be captivated as we unravel the secrets of the historic center, taking you on a fascinating journey through its storied past and vibrant present. Whether you're a history buff, an architecture enthusiast, or simply a curious traveler, the treasures of Salzburg's historic center await your exploration.

information on each landmark: history, significance, and practical tips

1. Salzburg Cathedral (Dom):

The Salzburg Cathedral, also known as Dom, is a masterpiece of Baroque architecture and one of the city's most iconic landmarks. Here's some detailed information on this magnificent site:

- **History:** The construction of the Salzburg Cathedral began in 1614 and was completed in 1628. It stands on the site of earlier churches, with the first recorded church dating back to 774. Over the centuries, the cathedral underwent several renovations and additions, resulting in its current grandeur.

- **Significance:** The Salzburg Cathedral holds great historical and religious significance. It served as the church of the Archbishops of Salzburg and is dedicated to Saint Rupert, the patron saint of the city. The cathedral has witnessed important events, including the baptism of Wolfgang Amadeus Mozart.

- **Architecture:** The cathedral's exterior features impressive domes, towers, and intricate Baroque details. Step inside to admire the stunning interior, adorned with marble, gold accents, and vibrant frescoes. Don't miss the chance to see the famous organ, which dates back to 1704 and is one of the oldest playable organs in the world.

- **Practical Tips for Visiting:** When visiting the Salzburg Cathedral, remember to dress appropriately, as it is a place of worship. Admission to the cathedral is free, but there may be a small fee to access the towers for panoramic views. Check the opening hours, as they may vary. Guided tours are available for those interested in a deeper exploration of the cathedral's history and architecture.

2. Hohensalzburg Fortress:

- *History*: Hohensalzburg Fortress is one of Europe's largest and best-preserved medieval fortresses, with origins dating back to the 11th century.

- *Significance:* It served as a residence, military stronghold, and symbol of power for the ruling Prince-Archbishops of Salzburg.

- *Architecture:* The fortress exhibits impressive medieval architecture, with fortified walls, courtyards, and a variety of structures, including the Fortress Museum.

  - *Practical Tips for Visiting:* Accessible by funicular or a steep hike. Enjoy stunning views of the city from the towers. Explore the fortress's various attractions, including the Marionette Museum.

3. *Mirabell Palace and Gardens:*

  - *History:* Built in 1606, Mirabell Palace served as the residence of the Prince-Archbishops and now houses municipal offices.

  - *Significance:* The palace and its gardens exemplify Italian Baroque design and are known for their aesthetic beauty and cultural importance.

  - *Architecture:* The palace features elegant facades and ornate interiors. The gardens display symmetrical patterns, fountains, statues, and vibrant flowerbeds.

  - *Practical Tips for Visiting:* Take a leisurely stroll through the gardens and enjoy the serene atmosphere. Attend concerts in the Marble Hall or visit the palace's municipal offices.

4. Getreidegasse:

  - *History:* Getreidegasse is Salzburg's most famous shopping street, with origins dating back to the Middle Ages.

  - *Significance:* It is renowned for its historic architecture, lively atmosphere, and as the birthplace of Wolfgang Amadeus Mozart.

  - *Architecture:* The street is lined with charming townhouses adorned with wrought-iron signs and features a mix of shops, boutiques, and cafes.

  - *Practical Tips for Visiting:* Explore the unique shops offering traditional crafts, fashion, and local delicacies. Visit Mozart's Birthplace and immerse yourself in the vibrant ambiance.

5. Mozart's Residence:

- *History:* Mozart's Residence, located on Makartplatz, was the family home of the Mozart family from 1773 to 1787.

- *Significance:* The residence provides insights into the life and works of Wolfgang Amadeus Mozart, one of the world's greatest composers.

- *Exhibits*: Explore the original instruments, memorabilia, and interactive displays that bring Mozart's life and musical genius to life.

- *Practical Tips for Visiting:* Engage with the exhibits to learn about Mozart's life and music. Check for any special events or concerts taking place at the residence.

6. Salzburg Museum:

- *History:* The Salzburg Museum, housed in the Neue Residenz building, offers a comprehensive collection showcasing Salzburg's history and culture.

- *Significance:* It provides a deeper understanding of Salzburg's heritage, art, music, and architectural contributions.

- *Exhibits:* The museum features a range of exhibits covering prehistoric times to the present day, including artifacts, artworks, and multimedia displays.

- *Practical Tips for Visiting:* Plan your visit to explore the specific exhibitions that interest you the most. Consider guided tours for a curated experience.

Sound of Music Sites: Reliving the Movie Magic

Get ready to relive the magic of the beloved film "The Sound of Music" as we take you on a journey to discover the iconic sites that captured the hearts of audiences worldwide. Explore the enchanting locations where the von Trapp family's story unfolded and immerse yourself in the captivating landscapes of Salzburg.

1. Mirabell Gardens:

Step into the picturesque Mirabell Gardens, where Maria and the von Trapp children danced and sang their way through the iconic song "Do-Re-Mi." Marvel at the vibrant flowerbeds, graceful statues, and the famous Pegasus Fountain. Let the melodies of the film guide you as you retrace the footsteps of the von Trapp family in this stunning setting.

2. Nonnberg Abbey:

Visit Nonnberg Abbey, the real-life convent where the character of Maria was a novice. This historic abbey provided the backdrop for Maria's enchanting wedding scene in the film. Take a moment to appreciate the abbey's beautiful architecture and soak in the serene atmosphere that inspired this timeless story.

3. Mondsee:

Embark on a journey to the charming town of Mondsee, where the von Trapp wedding was filmed. Explore the picturesque Mondsee Abbey, which served as the setting for Maria and Captain von Trapp's nuptials. Take in the breathtaking views of Lake Mondsee and discover the quaint streets that transport you back to the magic of the film.

4. Leopoldskron Palace:

Discover the iconic Leopoldskron Palace, the enchanting exterior of the von Trapp family home in the movie. Admire the majestic beauty of this lakeside palace, set against the backdrop of the stunning Leopoldskroner Weiher lake. While access to the interior may be limited, the exterior alone is a testament to the film's enduring legacy.

5. Hellbrunn Palace:

Explore the whimsical Hellbrunn Palace, home to the charming gazebo featured in the song "Sixteen Going on Seventeen." Wander through the palace's grounds, delight in the trick fountains, and imagine the romantic scenes that unfolded within the gazebo's walls. Immerse yourself in the nostalgia and charm of this remarkable filming location.

6. Salzburg Old Town:

Although not directly featured in the film, Salzburg's Old Town provides a captivating backdrop that captures the spirit of "The Sound of Music." Take a leisurely stroll through the cobblestone streets, admire the historic architecture, and uncover hidden gems that exude the same enchantment depicted in the movie.

As you visit these Sound of Music sites, allow the melodies and memories of the film to guide your experience. Whether you're a devoted fan or simply appreciate the beauty of these locations, reliving the movie magic in Salzburg is a truly unforgettable experience. Remember to check for any guided tours or special events that may enhance your visit and provide deeper insights into the making of this timeless cinematic masterpiece.

Off the Beaten Path: Hidden Treasures and Local Delights

While Salzburg is renowned for its famous landmarks and film locations, the city holds many hidden treasures and local delights that are off the beaten path. In this chapter, we invite you to venture beyond the well-trodden tourist routes and discover the lesser-known gems that showcase the authentic charm and unique character of Salzburg.

1. Steingasse:

Step into the enchanting Steingasse, one of Salzburg's oldest and most charming streets. This narrow lane is lined with historic buildings, quaint shops, and cozy cafes. Wander through its atmospheric alleys, immerse yourself in the centuries-old architecture, and soak up the local ambiance.

2. Linzergasse:

Explore the vibrant Linzergasse, a bustling street that offers a blend of history, culture, and culinary delights. Stroll along the pedestrian-friendly boulevard, browse the boutique shops, and stop by traditional bakeries to savor a freshly baked Linzer torte, a famous local pastry.

3. Augustiner Brewery:

Experience a true taste of Salzburg at the Augustiner Brewery, a hidden gem loved by locals. This historic brewery, located in the Mülln district, features a traditional beer garden where you can enjoy a refreshing mug of locally brewed beer. Pair it with hearty Austrian cuisine served in the brewery's halls filled with communal tables and a lively atmosphere.

4. St. Sebastian Cemetery:

Discover the peaceful and atmospheric St. Sebastian Cemetery, a hidden oasis of tranquility. Wander among the ancient tombstones, admire the beautiful sculptures, and find solace in this serene space away from the bustling city. This cemetery holds historical significance and is the final resting place of many notable Salzburg residents.

5. Museum der Moderne:

For art enthusiasts seeking contemporary works, visit the Museum der Moderne located atop the Mönchsberg. This modern art museum boasts an impressive collection of paintings, sculptures, and installations from both Austrian and international artists. Enjoy the breathtaking views of the city from the museum terrace while immersing yourself in the world of modern art.

6. Bürgerspital St. Blasius:

Experience the cultural heritage of Salzburg at the Bürgerspital St. Blasius. This historic building houses a pharmacy, museum, and restaurant. Explore the museum to learn about the history of the Bürgerspital and its charitable mission, and savor traditional Austrian dishes made from locally sourced ingredients at the restaurant.

7. Gaisberg:

Escape the hustle and bustle of the city and venture to Gais-berg, the local's favorite mountain. Embark on a hike or take a leisurely drive to the summit, where breathtaking panoramic views of Salzburg and the surrounding alpine landscape await. Enjoy outdoor activities like paragliding or simply bask in the natural beauty of this hidden gem.

These off-the-beaten-path destinations offer a glimpse into the authentic side of Salzburg, away from the crowds. Embrace the local atmosphere, savor traditional flavors, and uncover the hidden treasures that make Salzburg a truly remarkable destination. By venturing off the beaten path, you'll create lasting memories and gain a deeper appreciation for the city's rich culture and hidden delights.

II

Part Two

Immersing in Salzburg's Musical Legacy

Chapter 4

The Mozart Trail: Tracing the Footsteps of a Genius

Mozart's Birthplace: Journey into the Maestro's Childhood

I mmerse yourself in the life and legacy of one of the world's greatest composers, Wolfgang Amadeus Mozart, as we take you on a captivating journey through his childhood. In this chapter, we'll explore Mozart's Birthplace, a place of immense historical significance where the musical genius first saw the light of day.

1. History:

Mozart's Birthplace, located in the heart of Salzburg's Getreidegasse, is a yellow townhouse where Wolfgang Amadeus Mozart was born on January 27, 1756. The house, known as "Mozarts Geburtshaus," has been carefully preserved to provide visitors with a glimpse into the world in which Mozart grew up.

2. Museum:

Step inside the birthplace and embark on a fascinating tour of the Mozart family's former residence. The museum, spread across three floors, showcases an extensive collection of memorabilia, original instruments, family portraits, handwritten compositions, and personal artifacts that provide insights into the life and works of Mozart.

3. Childhood and Early Life:

Explore the rooms where Mozart spent his formative years and gain a deeper understanding of his prodigious talent and musical upbringing. Visit the room where he was born, see the Mozart family's living quarters, and imagine the melodies that filled these walls during his early years.

4. Exhibits and Interactive Displays:

The museum features interactive displays that bring Mozart's music to life. Listen to his compositions, learn about his musical development, and gain a deeper appreciation for his remarkable contributions to classical music. Engage with hands-on exhibits that allow you to explore the world of 18th-century music and try your hand at composing.

5. Special Events and Performances:

Keep an eye out for special events and performances held at Mozart's Birthplace. Experience live concerts showcasing Mozart's music, lectures by musicologists, and demonstrations of period instruments, providing an immersive and enriching experience for visitors.

6. Getreidegasse:

After exploring Mozart's Birthplace, take a leisurely stroll along Getreidegasse. Admire the charming facades, wrought-iron signs, and traditional shops. Pause at No. 9, where the

Mozart family resided until Mozart's early teenage years, and appreciate the historical significance of this vibrant street.

Visiting Mozart's Birthplace is a unique opportunity to delve into the early life and musical genius of Wolfgang Amadeus Mozart. Gain insight into his extraordinary talent, his family dynamics, and the influences that shaped his remarkable career. From original manuscripts to personal belongings, the museum offers a fascinating journey through the life and times of one of history's greatest composers.

Prepare to be captivated by the musical heritage that resonates within the walls of Mozart's Birthplace, and let the melodies of his genius guide you through this extraordinary chapter of Salzburg's rich cultural tapestry.

Mozartplatz and Mozarteum: A Tribute to a Musical Prodigy

Continue your exploration of Mozart's footsteps as we visit Mozartplatz and Mozarteum, two remarkable landmarks that pay tribute to the enduring legacy of the musical prodigy, Wolfgang Amadeus Mozart.

1. Mozartplatz:

Located in the heart of Salzburg's historic center, Mozartplatz is a vibrant square dedicated to celebrating Mozart's life and achievements. Here's what you can expect to discover:

- **Mozart Monument:** Marvel at the grand statue of Mozart standing proudly in the center of Mozartplatz. Crafted by sculptor Ludwig Schwanthaler, this iconic monument serves as a timeless symbol of Salzburg's connection to its musical genius.

- **Surrounding Architecture:** Take in the architectural beauty surrounding Mozartplatz. Admire the elegant buildings with their ornate facades, reflecting the charm of Salzburg's historic atmosphere.

- **Festivals and Events:** Mozartplatz serves as a gathering place for various festivals and events that celebrate Mozart's music and influence. Keep an eye out for open-air concerts, performances, and cultural festivities that enliven the square throughout the year.

2. Mozarteum:

Just a short walk from Mozartplatz, you'll find the Mozarteum, a prestigious institution dedicated to music education and the preservation of Mozart's legacy. Explore the following highlights:

- **History and Mission:** Discover the rich history of the Mozarteum, which was founded in 1841 with the aim of fostering musical excellence. Learn about its commitment to Mozart's works and the promotion of music education.

- **Mozarteum University:** Gain insight into one of the world's leading music universities, the Mozarteum University Salzburg. This renowned institution offers comprehensive music programs and nurtures young talent from around the globe.

– *Concerts and Performances:* Experience the magic of live performances at the Mozarteum. Attend concerts featuring talented musicians, orchestras, and vocalists who bring Mozart's music to life within the walls of this esteemed institution.

– *Mozart's Residence:* Visit the neighboring building, which was once Mozart's residence. While it is not open to the public, the historical significance of this place adds to the overall ambiance and appreciation of Mozart's connection to Salzburg.

Immerse yourself in the spirit of Mozart as you explore Mozartplatz and Mozarteum. Reflect on the profound impact of his music and the lasting influence he has had on the world of classical composition. These landmarks serve as a testament to Mozart's enduring legacy and his deep-rooted connection to the city of Salzburg.

Take a moment to absorb the atmosphere, listen to his melodies resonating in your mind, and pay tribute to the genius whose contributions continue to inspire generations of musicians and music lovers.

Salzburg Marionette Theatre: Captivating Performances for All Ages

Step into a world of enchantment and wonder at the Salzburg Marionette Theatre, a cherished institution that brings stories to life through the artistry of puppetry. Experience captivating performances that delight audiences of all ages and celebrate the rich tradition of marionette theater in Salzburg.

1. History of the Salzburg Marionette Theatre:
Discover the fascinating history of the Salzburg Marionette Theatre, which dates back to 1913. Learn about the dedication and craftsmanship that has preserved this unique form of theater throughout the years, making it one of the oldest and most renowned marionette theaters in the world.

2. Intimate Theater Setting:
Enter the intimate theater and feel the anticipation build as the curtain rises. The cozy setting allows for an up-close and personal experience, enabling you to witness the intricate movements and artistry of the marionettes as they take center stage.

3. Diverse Repertoire:
Be captivated by a diverse repertoire that spans classic operas, ballets, musicals, and fairy tales. Experience the magic of watching beloved characters come to life through the expert manipulation of the marionettes, accompanied by beautiful music and elaborate sets.

4. Skillful Puppetry and Artistry:

Marvel at the skillful puppetry and artistry displayed by the puppeteers, who bring each marionette to life with precision and grace. Admire the intricately designed puppets, from their exquisite costumes to their meticulously crafted movements, as they tell stories with remarkable expressiveness.

5. Performances for All Ages:

The Salzburg Marionette Theatre offers performances that cater to audiences of all ages. From whimsical fairy tales that ignite the imagination of young viewers to classic operas that enchant music enthusiasts, there is something for everyone to enjoy. Experience the joy of shared moments and the universality of storytelling that transcends age boundaries.

6. Cultural Heritage and Educational Programs:

Recognized as an integral part of Salzburg's cultural heritage, the Salzburg Marionette Theatre also offers educational programs and workshops. Delve deeper into the art of marionette theater, learn about the history of puppetry, and even try your hand at manipulating puppets under the guidance of skilled professionals.

Immerse yourself in the magic of the Salzburg Marionette Theatre, where the art of puppetry takes center stage. Prepare to be transported to imaginary worlds, captivated by the skill and craftsmanship of the puppeteers, and moved by the timeless stories brought to life through the enchanting medium of marionettes.

Whether you are a fan of theater, a lover of music, or simply seeking a unique and memorable cultural experience, a visit to the Salzburg Marionette Theatre promises to be a truly captivating journey into the realm of puppetry and storytelling.

Salzburg Festival: A Melodic Extravaganza

Prepare to be swept away by the grandeur and artistry of the Salzburg Festival, a world-renowned celebration of music and performing arts. Experience an immersive melodic extravaganza that brings together esteemed artists, captivating performances, and the stunning backdrop of Salzburg's cultural heritage.

1. History and Legacy:

Discover the rich history and enduring legacy of the Salzburg Festival, which was founded in 1920. Learn about its origins, vision, and commitment to showcasing the finest classical music, opera, theater, and dance performances.

2. Diverse Program:

Immerse yourself in a diverse program that spans a multitude of genres and art forms. From stirring opera productions to symphonic concerts, from innovative theater performances to mesmerizing ballets, the Salzburg Festival offers a wide array of artistic experiences that cater to all tastes.

3. Iconic Venues:

Witness performances in iconic venues that form the backdrop for these artistic masterpieces. From the majestic Salzburg Festival Hall to the historic Felsenreitschule and the intimate Haus für Mozart, each venue contributes to the unique atmosphere and enhances the magic of the performances.

4. Acclaimed Artists:

Experience the virtuosity of internationally renowned artists who grace the stages of the Salzburg Festival. From world-class conductors and orchestras to acclaimed opera singers, actors, and dancers, the festival showcases talent of the highest caliber, ensuring unforgettable performances that leave audiences in awe.

5. Cultural Immersion:

The Salzburg Festival is not just about the performances; it is a celebration of Salzburg's rich cultural heritage. Immerse yourself in the city's historic charm, explore its architectural wonders, and savor the culinary delights that complement the festival experience. The city comes alive with a vibrant energy and a sense of artistic fervor.

6. Events and Highlights:

Keep an eye out for special events and highlights that make the Salzburg Festival even more memorable. From open-air performances at the iconic Cathedral Square to screenings of operas and concerts in public spaces, there are opportunities for everyone to engage with the festival's spirit.

Indulge your senses and let the melodic extravaganza of the Salzburg Festival transport you to a realm of artistic brilliance. Immerse yourself in the captivating performances, bask in the cultural richness of Salzburg, and join fellow music enthusiasts in celebrating the beauty and power of the performing arts.

Whether you are a seasoned festival-goer or attending for the first time, the Salzburg Festival promises an unforgettable experience that will leave you with cherished memories and a deep appreciation for the transformative power of music and the arts.

III

Part Three

Experiencing Salzburg Like a Local

Chapter 5

Beyond Mozart: Salzburg's Vibrant Music Scene

Salzburg Cathedral: Heavenly Notes in Sacred Surroundings

S tep into the rich musical tapestry of Salzburg beyond Mozart as we explore the magnificent Salzburg Cathedral. Immerse yourself in the heavenly notes that resonate within its sacred surroundings and discover the vibrant music scene that thrives within this architectural masterpiece.

1. History and Architecture:
Uncover the fascinating history of Salzburg Cathedral, a masterpiece of Baroque architecture that dates back to the 17th century. Marvel at the grandeur of its exterior, adorned with domes, towers, and intricate details, and step inside to be awed by the breathtaking beauty of its interior.

2. Musical Significance:
Salzburg Cathedral has been a focal point for music throughout its history, hosting countless concerts, performances, and

religious ceremonies. Experience the acoustics that have cap-tured the hearts of musicians and audiences alike, and imagine the sublime melodies that have filled this sacred space for centuries.

3. Organ:

Take a moment to admire the renowned organ of Salzburg Cathedral, one of the largest and most impressive in Europe. Discover its rich tones and intricate craftsmanship, and be transported by the majestic sounds that emanate from this extraordinary instrument during organ recitals and religious services.

4. Sacred Music Performances:

Attend a sacred music performance within the hallowed walls of Salzburg Cathedral and experience the transcendence of music in this divine setting. Be moved by the voices of renowned choirs and soloists as they fill the cathedral with their melodic interpretations of religious works, offering a deeply spiritual and uplifting experience.

5. Religious Services:

Participate in a religious service at Salzburg Cathedral and witness the fusion of music and spirituality. Allow the choral chants, hymns, and liturgical music to envelop you in a sense of reverence and connect with the centuries-old tradition of worship that continues to resonate within these sacred walls.

6. Seasonal Music Events:

Discover the diverse program of seasonal music events that take place at Salzburg Cathedral. From Christmas concerts that celebrate the joyous season to Easter performances that com-memorate the resurrection, these events offer unique oppor-tunities to experience the cathedral's musical heritage during special times of the year.

Salzburg Cathedral stands as a testament to the city's rich musi-cal legacy, inviting visitors to bask in the awe-inspiring beauty of its architecture and immerse themselves in the heavenly notes that permeate its sacred surroundings. Whether you attend a sacred music performance, participate in a religious service, or simply take a moment to appreciate the profound musical history within these walls, Salzburg Cathedral offers a truly extraordinary musical experience that goes beyond Mozart, showcasing the vibrant music scene that thrives in this remarkable city.

Salzburg Concert Halls: Venues for Memorable Performances

Step into the world of captivating performances as we explore the renowned concert halls of Salzburg. From opulent historic venues to modern architectural marvels, these halls provide the perfect settings for unforgettable musical experiences.

1. Great Festival Hall (Großes Festspielhaus):

Immerse yourself in the grandeur of the Great Festival Hall, a masterpiece of modern architecture. This prestigious venue, known for its exceptional acoustics, hosts world-class orches-tras, opera productions, and renowned soloists. Prepare to be enthralled by the breathtaking performances that grace this iconic stage.

2. Mozarteum University Concert Hall:

Discover the Mozarteum University Concert Hall, a venue that combines historical charm with exceptional musical performances. Home to the Mozarteum Orchestra Salzburg, this hall showcases the talents of emerging musicians and renowned guest artists. Experience the intimacy of this venue and be captivated by the exquisite interpretations of classical and contemporary works.

3. Haus für Mozart:

Enter the elegant Haus für Mozart, a theater dedicated to opera and theater productions. This historic venue, beautifully restored to its former glory, hosts performances that range from traditional operas to avant-garde productions. Prepare to be transported into the world of dramatic storytelling and exceptional vocal artistry.

4. Mirabell Palace and Palace Concerts:

Indulge in the enchantment of classical music at Mirabell Palace, where Palace Concerts take place in the opulent Marble Hall. Sit back and be serenaded by renowned ensembles as they perform masterpieces from Mozart and other classical composers. Let the majestic surroundings and sublime music create an unforgettable evening.

5. Salzburg Marionette Theatre:

While renowned for its marionette performances, the Salzburg Marionette Theatre also serves as an intimate concert venue. Experience unique chamber music concerts in this charming setting, where talented musicians showcase their skills alongside the magical artistry of marionette theater.

6. Salzburg Congress:

Discover the versatile Salzburg Congress, a modern congress and concert center that hosts a variety of performances. From classical concerts to jazz, pop, and contemporary performances, this venue accommodates diverse musical genres and ensures a memorable experience for audiences of all tastes.

The concert halls of Salzburg offer not only extraordinary performances but also a glimpse into the city's rich musical heritage. From the resounding acoustics of the Great Festival Hall to the intimate settings of the Mozarteum University Concert Hall and the Salzburg Marionette Theatre, each venue contributes to the vibrant music scene that thrives in this city.

Whether you attend a grand orchestral performance, a captivating opera, or an intimate chamber concert, these concert halls provide the perfect backdrop for exceptional musical experiences. Allow the harmonies to resonate within you, and let the talents of the performers transport you to new realms of musical expression, creating memories that will last a lifetime.

Jazz Clubs and Live Music: Exploring Salzburg's Rhythmic Soul

Prepare to be swept away by the pulsating rhythms and soulful melodies that echo through the jazz clubs and live music venues of Salzburg. In this chapter, we invite you to immerse yourself in the city's vibrant music scene, where the spirit of improvisation and the joy of live performances thrive.

1. Jazzit: Where Jazz Comes to Life

Step into the heart of Salzburg's jazz scene at Jazzit, an intimate and atmospheric club that sets the stage for mesmerizing performances. Experience the artistry and passion of both local talents and international jazz artists as they weave their musical magic. From smooth jazz to bluesy notes and funky grooves, Jazzit offers an immersive jazz experience that will leave you captivated.

2. Republic: A Fusion of Sounds

Discover Republic, a dynamic venue that celebrates the diversity of live music. Embrace the energy of this eclectic space as you explore a vibrant tapestry of musical genres. From jazz ensembles to indie bands and electronic acts, Republic delivers an ever-changing lineup that invites you to dance, groove, and revel in the spirited ambiance.

3. ARGEkultur: Exploring Musical Boundaries

Step into the world of ARGEkultur, a cultural center that pushes artistic boundaries and champions innovative musical expressions. Embark on a journey of discovery as you witness an array of genres, from jazz to world music and experimental sounds. ARGEkultur is a haven for both established and emerging artists, offering a platform for creativity and exploration.

4. Shamrock: Music and Merriment

Experience the vibrant spirit of Shamrock, a lively pub that not only brings an Irish atmosphere to Salzburg but also hosts live music events. Immerse yourself in the sounds of folk, acoustic, and rock performances that fill the air with lively energy. Join in the merry sing-alongs or simply enjoy the camaraderie and joviality that music brings.

5. Jazz Brunch and Festivals: Celebrating the Melodic Brunch

Indulge in the delightful combination of live jazz music and delectable cuisine at Salzburg's jazz brunches and festivals. Delight your senses with a harmonious Sunday brunch experience where talented musicians set the melodic backdrop for your culinary journey. Throughout the year, festivals dedicated to jazz music bring together a constellation of international and local artists, showcasing the rich diversity and creativity of the genre.

6. Music Bars and Cafés: Intimate Musical Hideaways

Discover Salzburg's hidden gems – the cozy music bars and cafés that offer intimate settings for live music performances. Allow yourself to be swept away by the acoustic singer-songwriters, small jazz ensembles, and soulful melodies that fill the air. Relax, savor a drink, and connect with the artists on a personal level as you immerse yourself in the intimate charm of these venues.

Salzburg's jazz clubs and live music scene offer a vibrant and diverse experience that complements the city's classical music heritage. Prepare to be enchanted by the improvisations, captivated by the raw talent of musicians, and moved by the collective energy shared between performers and audiences. Whether you're a seasoned jazz enthusiast or a curious explorer, Salzburg's rhythmic soul will leave an indelible mark on your musical journey.

Music Museums and Exhibitions: Unveiling the Melodic Artistry

Embark on a captivating journey through the music museums and exhibitions of Salzburg, where the rich tapestry of melodic artistry is unveiled. Explore the fascinating world of musical instruments, compositions, and the lives of renowned composers, as you gain a deeper appreciation for the creative spirit that has shaped Salzburg's musical heritage.

1. Mozarts Wohnhaus: The Life of Mozart

Step into Mozarts Wohnhaus, the former residence of the Mozart family, and immerse yourself in the life and works of the musical genius, Wolfgang Amadeus Mozart. Explore the meticulously preserved rooms, which house an impressive collection of artifacts, including original instruments, hand-written compositions, and personal memorabilia. Gain insights into Mozart's remarkable journey and his enduring impact on classical music.

2. Salzburg Museum: A Symphony of Salzburg's History

Discover the Salzburg Museum, a treasure trove of historical artifacts that includes a dedicated section to the city's musical heritage. Unveil the stories of Salzburg's illustrious composers, including Mozart, through exhibits that showcase their lives, influences, and contributions to the world of music. Immerse yourself in the cultural context of their times and witness the evolution of Salzburg's musical landscape.

3. House of Music: Interactive Musical Exploration

Experience the interactive wonders of the House of Music, a museum dedicated to the exploration and celebration of sound and music. Engage with innovative exhibits that invite you to play musical instruments, experiment with compositions, and delve into the science behind sound. Immerse yourself in the interactive installations and discover the joy of music through a multi-sensory journey.

4. Carolino Augusteum Museum: The Art of Instrument Making

Delve into the art of instrument making at the Carolino Augusteum Museum, which houses an exceptional collection of historical instruments. Admire the craftsmanship and precision that went into creating these masterpieces as you explore the evolution of musical instruments throughout history. Gain a deeper understanding of the technical and artistic aspects that shape the world of music.

5. Mirabell Palace: Resonating Melodies

Marvel at the musical wonders within Mirabell Palace, where you can explore the exquisite Marble Hall and its musical history. Discover the Palace Concerts, which showcase talented musicians performing classical masterpieces in this opulent setting.

Let the harmonies resonate through the walls, transporting you to an era of refined elegance and melodic enchantment.

6. Special Exhibitions and Temporary Installations:

Stay informed about special exhibitions and temporary installations that showcase the dynamic and ever-evolving world of music. From thematic exhibitions that delve into specific genres or composers to immersive multimedia experiences that push the boundaries of traditional displays, these temporary offerings provide fresh perspectives on the melodic artistry of Salzburg.

Unveil the melodic artistry of Salzburg through its music museums and exhibitions, and witness the transformative power of music across time and space. Immerse yourself in the lives of composers, explore the intricacies of musical instruments, and engage with interactive installations that ignite your own creative spirit. Discover the stories, sounds, and symphonies that have shaped Salzburg's vibrant music scene, and deepen your connection to the melodic artistry that transcends boundaries.

Chapter 6

Savoring Salzburg : Culinary Delights and Traditional Tastes

Traditional Austrian Cuisine: Delightful Dishes and Local Specialties

P repare your taste buds for a delectable journey into the world of traditional Austrian cuisine as we explore the delightful dishes and local specialties that define Salzburg's culinary landscape. From hearty comfort foods to mouthwatering pastries, embark on a gastronomic adventure that will leave you craving for more.

1. Schnitzel: Crispy and Tender Delight

Indulge in the quintessential Austrian dish – the Schnitzel. Immerse yourself in the symphony of flavors as you savor the crispy breaded exterior that encases a tender and juicy meat, usually veal or pork. Accompanied by a squeeze of lemon and a side of potato salad or warm buttery spaetzle, Schnitzel is a culinary masterpiece that embodies Austrian comfort food.

2. Tafelspitz: A Royal Feast

Experience the regal flavors of Tafelspitz, a classic Austrian dish fit for royalty. This succulent boiled beef is simmered to perfection with aromatic spices and served with an array of traditional accompaniments such as horseradish sauce, apple-horseradish compote, and crispy roasted potatoes. Let the tender meat melt in your mouth as you savor the richness of this time-honored delicacy.

3. Kaspressknödel: Cheesy Dumplings

Delight in the hearty and comforting Kaspressknödel, a savory dumpling made with a blend of melted cheese, onions, and herbs. Served in a flavorful broth or accompanied by sauerkraut, these cheesy delights are a favorite among locals and offer a taste of true Austrian comfort cuisine. Experience the combination of textures and flavors that make Kaspressknödel a true delight.

4. Salzburger Nockerl: Sweet Soufflé Delicacy

Indulge your sweet tooth with Salzburger Nockerl, a fluffy and delicate soufflé that embodies the essence of Salzburg's dessert culture. Made with whisked egg whites, powdered sugar, and a touch of vanilla, this cloud-like confection is baked to perfection and served with a sprinkling of powdered sugar. Let each heavenly bite transport you to a realm of sweet enchantment.

5. Apple Strudel: A Slice of Delight

Sample the iconic Apple Strudel, a beloved Austrian pastry that showcases the harmony of tart apples, delicate pastry layers, and warm spices. Experience the flaky crust and the comforting aroma of cinnamon as you savor each bite. Pair it with a dollop of vanilla ice cream or a drizzle of warm vanilla sauce for the ultimate indulgence.

6. Mozartkugel: A Musical Confection

Discover the Mozartkugel, a sweet treat that pays homage to Salzburg's most famous musical son, Wolfgang Amadeus Mozart. These round chocolate-covered marzipan and nougat confections are a symphony of flavors and textures. Take a bite and let the harmonious blend of chocolate and marzipan dance on your taste buds, celebrating the melodic legacy of Mozart.

Immerse yourself in the culinary delights of traditional Austrian cuisine, where flavors and traditions intertwine to create a truly unforgettable dining experience. From the savory satisfaction of Schnitzel to the sweet indulgence of Mozartkugel, each dish tells a story of Salzburg's rich culinary heritage. Allow your taste buds to savor the unique flavors and textures, and embrace the pleasure of savoring Salzburg's traditional tastes.

Coffeehouses and Patisseries: Indulging in Sweet Pleasures

Awaken your senses and treat yourself to the sweet pleasures of Salzburg's coffeehouses and patisseries. Step into a world of rich aromas, exquisite pastries, and the comforting embrace of a perfectly brewed cup of coffee. Delight in the artistry and craftsmanship of these establishments as they invite you to indulge in moments of pure culinary bliss.

1. Café Tomaselli: A Historic Gem

Experience the timeless elegance of Café Tomaselli, one of Salzburg's oldest coffeehouses. Delight in the refined ambiance as you sip your coffee and savor delectable pastries that have been perfected over generations. Let the rich history and the comforting atmosphere transport you to a bygone era of sophistication and refined taste.

2. Café Fürst: Home of the Original Mozartkugel

Pay a visit to Café Fürst, the birthplace of the Original Mozartkugel. Indulge in this iconic chocolate and marzipan confection that has delighted taste buds for over a century. Pair it with a cup of aromatic coffee and let the harmonious flavors dance on your palate as you immerse yourself in the sweet legacy of Salzburg's most famous musical son.

3. Patisserie 5020: Modern Delights with a Twist

Discover Patisserie 5020, a contemporary patisserie that infuses traditional flavors with a modern twist. Allow your taste buds to be tantalized by an array of innovative pastries, from delicate macarons to luscious tarts and artistic cakes. Indulge in the creative combinations and the exquisite presentation that make each bite a moment of pure culinary delight.

4. Café Bazar: Lakeside Charm

Enjoy the lakeside charm of Café Bazar, nestled along the banks of the Salzach River. Take in the panoramic views while sipping your coffee and savoring homemade pastries that tempt with their enticing aromas. Allow the relaxed atmosphere and the gentle breeze to transport you to a haven of tranquility and sweet indulgence.

5. Café-Konditorei Fürst: Time-Honored Traditions

Experience the artistry and craftsmanship of Café-Konditorei Fürst, a family-run establishment that upholds time-honored traditions. Be captivated by the enticing display of beautifully crafted pastries and cakes, each a work of edible art. Treat yourself to a slice of culinary perfection and let the flavors unfold in a symphony of taste.

6. Bäckerei-Konditorei Friesacher: Local Delicacies

Explore the local delicacies at Bäckerei-Konditorei Friesacher, a beloved bakery and patisserie that delights with its wide array of sweet treats. Indulge in traditional Austrian pastries, such as Linzer Torte, Esterházy Torte, and Bienenstich, each showcasing the region's culinary heritage. Experience the passion and dedication that go into crafting these mouthwatering delights.

Salzburg's coffeehouses and patisseries offer a haven for those seeking a moment of respite and indulgence. Let the aroma of freshly brewed coffee envelop you as you surrender to the allure of tempting pastries. Each establishment tells its own story, inviting you to experience the art of coffee and pastry-making in its most refined form. Savor the sweetness, relish the flavors, and allow yourself to be transported to a world of pure culinary pleasure in Salzburg's charming coffeehouses and patisseries.

Salzburg Beer Culture: Raising a Glass to Local Brews

Immerse yourself in the vibrant beer culture of Salzburg, where centuries-old traditions blend with innovative brewing techniques to create a truly unique and flavorful experience. From traditional beer halls to craft breweries, join in the celebration of Salzburg's rich brewing heritage and raise a glass to the art of beer craftsmanship.

1. Augustiner Bräustübl: A Historic Beer Hall

Step into the iconic Augustiner Bräustübl, a historic beer hall that dates back to the 17th century. Bask in the convivial atmosphere as you sample their renowned house-brewed beers, served straight from wooden barrels. Enjoy the camaraderie of communal seating, savor traditional Bavarian pretzels, and toast to the flavors of Salzburg's brewing tradition.

2. Stiegl-Brauwelt: The Art of Brewing

Discover the art of brewing at Stiegl-Brauwelt, a modern brewery that offers an interactive and educational experience. Embark on a brewery tour to learn about the brewing process, from the selection of ingredients to the fermentation and bottling. Indulge in a tasting session, where you can savor a range of Stiegl beers, each showcasing the brewery's commitment to quality and craftsmanship.

3. Beer Gardens: Nature's Cheers

Experience the joy of a beer garden, where you can savor your favorite brews amidst lush greenery and a relaxed atmosphere. Take a leisurely stroll along the banks of the Salzach River or in the Mirabell Gardens, and find a cozy spot to enjoy a cold beer while soaking in the beauty of Salzburg's natural surroundings. It's the perfect way to unwind and savor the moment.

4. Craft Breweries: Innovation in Every Sip

Embrace the creativity of Salzburg's craft breweries, where innovative brewers push the boundaries of traditional beer styles. Sample a variety of handcrafted brews that showcase unique flavors and unexpected combinations. From hoppy IPAs to rich stouts and refreshing fruit-infused beers, the craft beer scene in Salzburg offers something for every beer enthusiast.

5. Beer Tastings: A Journey of Flavors

Engage in beer tastings that take you on a journey of flavors and aromas. Join knowledgeable guides who will introduce you to the diverse range of Salzburg's beer offerings. Learn about different styles, brewing techniques, and food pairings as you explore the nuances and complexities of each beer. Expand your palate and deepen your appreciation for the artistry behind every sip.

6. Beer Festivals: Celebrating Sudsy Delights

Immerse yourself in the festive spirit of beer festivals that take place throughout the year in Salzburg. Join locals and visitors alike as they come together to celebrate the rich brewing heritage of the city. Raise your stein, enjoy live music, and revel in the convivial atmosphere of these joyous gatherings that highlight the best of Salzburg's beer culture.

Salzburg's beer culture invites you to savor the flavors, embrace the traditions, and immerse yourself in the conviviality of raising a glass to local brews. Whether you're enjoying a pint in a historic beer hall, exploring the art of brewing at a modern brewery, or discovering the innovative creations of craft breweries, each sip is a celebration of the rich beer heritage that flows through the city. Cheers to the vibrant beer culture of Salzburg, where every glass tells a story and every sip is an invitation to savor the craft of brewing.

Chapter 7

Shopping in Salzburg: Souvenirs and Unique Finds

Old Town Shopping: Boutiques, Crafts, and Fashion

Get ready to indulge in a shopping spree through Salzburg's enchanting Old Town, where charming boutiques, local crafts, and fashionable finds await. Immerse yourself in a world of unique treasures as you explore the cobblestone streets and discover hidden gems that reflect Salzburg's rich heritage and contemporary style.

1. Getreidegasse: Historic Charm and Fashionable Delights
   Stroll along Getreidegasse, Salzburg's iconic shopping street known for its historic charm and vibrant mix of local and international brands. Explore boutique shops offering stylish fashion, footwear, and accessories, as well as specialty stores showcasing exquisite jewelry, watches, and traditional Austrian clothing. Let the captivating ambiance and window displays inspire your shopping adventure.

2. Linzer Gasse: Artistic Crafts and Souvenirs

Discover Linzer Gasse, a bustling street lined with shops offering a delightful array of artistic crafts and unique souvenirs. Browse through stores featuring handcrafted ceramics, glassware, textiles, and woodwork, each reflecting the craftsmanship and creativity of Salzburg's artisans. Take home a piece of Salzburg's artistic heritage and find the perfect memento to cherish.

3. Goldgasse: Hidden Treasures and Curiosities

Uncover the hidden treasures and curiosities of Goldgasse, a narrow lane brimming with independent shops and ateliers. Delight in the eclectic mix of vintage finds, handmade accessories, quirky collectibles, and whimsical artworks. Allow yourself to be enchanted by the unexpected and embrace the thrill of discovering something truly unique.

4. Judengasse: Antique and Vintage Finds

Step into Judengasse, a street known for its antique and vintage shops that offer a glimpse into the past. Explore the curated collections of antique furniture, vintage clothing, books, and collectibles. Let the nostalgia and history of each item transport you to a bygone era as you uncover treasures that tell stories of Salzburg's rich cultural heritage.

5. Salzburg's Markets: Local Flavors and Crafts

Immerse yourself in the vibrant atmosphere of Salzburg's markets, where you can find an abundance of local flavors and crafts. Visit the bustling Salzburg Market at Universitätsplatz, offering fresh produce, regional delicacies, and artisanal products. Discover the Saturday Farmers' Market at Kajetanerplatz, showcasing organic goods, handmade crafts, and local artwork.

Experience the lively ambiance, engage with vendors, and savor the authentic essence of Salzburg.

6. Designer Boutiques and Concept Stores

Indulge in high-end fashion and design at Salzburg's designer boutiques and concept stores. Explore the offerings of renowned fashion houses, discover emerging designers, and find cutting-edge pieces that reflect Salzburg's contemporary style. From avant-garde fashion to curated home decor, these stores offer a unique shopping experience for the fashion-forward and design-conscious.

Salzburg's Old Town is a shopper's paradise, blending history, craftsmanship, and fashion-forward finds. Whether you're seeking fashionable attire, artistic crafts, antique treasures, or authentic souvenirs, the boutiques, specialty shops, and markets of Salzburg's Old Town promise an unforgettable shopping experience. Embrace the charm, immerse yourself in the local culture, and uncover hidden gems as you embark on a shopping adventure that reflects the unique spirit of Salzburg.

Traditional Markets: From Farmers' Fare to Antique Treasures

Immerse yourself in the vibrant atmosphere of Salzburg's traditional markets, where a treasure trove of delights awaits. From fresh local produce to handmade crafts and antique treasures, these markets offer a sensory experience that brings you closer to Salzburg's rich culture and heritage.

1. Salzburg Market at Universitätsplatz:

Explore the bustling Salzburg Market at Universitätsplatz, where a vibrant array of stalls awaits. Let your senses guide you as you wander through the colorful displays of fresh fruits, vegetables, aromatic herbs, and regional specialties. Engage with local vendors, sample artisanal cheeses, meats, and baked goods, and discover the flavors that define Salzburg's culinary landscape.

2. Saturday Farmers' Market at Kajetanerplatz:

Immerse yourself in the lively ambiance of the Saturday Farmers' Market at Kajetanerplatz. Indulge in the bounty of organic produce, locally sourced honey, homemade preserves, and freshly baked bread. Experience the community spirit as you chat with farmers and artisans, learning about their craft and the stories behind their products. This market is a true celebration of Salzburg's agricultural heritage.

3. Antique Markets and Flea Markets:

Delve into the world of antique treasures and vintage finds at Salzburg's antique and flea markets. Wander through stalls adorned with unique collectibles, timeless furniture, vintage clothing, and fascinating curiosities. Allow yourself to be captivated by the stories that each item holds and uncover hidden gems that reflect the charm of a bygone era.

4. Christmas Markets:

Experience the enchantment of Salzburg's magical Christmas markets, which come alive during the holiday season. Stroll through the beautifully decorated stalls, adorned with twinkling lights and the aroma of mulled wine and roasted chestnuts filling the air. Discover handcrafted ornaments, traditional crafts, and delightful treats, immersing yourself in the festive spirit of Salzburg.

5. Easter Markets:

Celebrate the arrival of spring at Salzburg's Easter markets, where the city comes alive with vibrant colors and festive cheer. Admire the intricately painted Easter eggs, browse through handcrafted gifts, and indulge in seasonal delights like Easter pastries and chocolates. Join in the joyful atmosphere as locals and visitors come together to embrace the traditions of Easter.

6. Artisan Markets and Craft Fairs:

Experience the creativity and craftsmanship of local artisans at Salzburg's artisan markets and craft fairs. Explore stalls featuring handmade jewelry, ceramics, textiles, and other unique creations. Engage with the artisans themselves, learning about their techniques and inspirations. Take home a one-of-a-kind piece that embodies the talent and artistry of Salzburg's skilled craftsmen and women.

Salzburg's traditional markets are a treasure trove of experiences, offering a glimpse into the city's rich heritage and the creativity of its artisans. Whether you're seeking fresh local produce, antique treasures, or handcrafted souvenirs, these markets provide a sensory journey that celebrates the flavors, craftsmanship, and cultural traditions of Salzburg. Immerse yourself in the vibrant energy, engage with local vendors, and uncover the hidden treasures that make each market visit a truly unforgettable experience.

Salzburg's Musical Souvenirs: Gifts for the Melody Enthusiasts

For the melody enthusiasts and music lovers, Salzburg offers a delightful array of musical souvenirs that capture the essence of the city's rich musical heritage. From Mozart-inspired mementos to classical music recordings and unique instruments, these gifts will enchant and inspire, allowing you to bring a piece of Salzburg's melodic magic home with you.

1. Mozart Memorabilia:

Celebrate the genius of Wolfgang Amadeus Mozart with a range of Mozart memorabilia. Explore shops offering Mozart-themed gifts such as keychains, magnets, t-shirts, and mugs adorned with his image. Consider acquiring a replica of Mozart's favorite instrument, the piano, or a miniature figurine that pays tribute to the musical maestro. These souvenirs serve as timeless reminders of Salzburg's most famous son.

2. Classical Music Recordings:

Immerse yourself in the world of classical music with a selection of recordings by renowned Salzburg-based orchestras and musicians. Look for CDs or vinyl records featuring performances of Mozart's masterpieces, as well as works by other notable composers who have graced Salzburg's stages. Relive the melodic enchantment of Salzburg's music scene and create a symphony of memories at home.

3. Musical Instruments and Accessories:

Explore specialty shops that offer a wide range of musical instruments and accessories. From high-quality violins and pianos to intricate music boxes and handcrafted woodwind instruments, these stores cater to musicians and music enthusiasts alike. Consider acquiring a small instrument or a piece of unique musical jewelry as a cherished memento that reflects your passion for music.

4. Sheet Music and Songbooks:

Delve into the musical scores that have shaped Salzburg's legacy by acquiring sheet music or songbooks. Whether you're a musician seeking to perform these timeless compositions or a collector interested in owning a piece of musical history, these stores offer a wide selection of scores, ranging from Mozart's symphonies and operas to works by other influential composers.

5. Music-themed Art and Decor:

Adorn your living space with music-themed art and decor that captures the spirit of Salzburg's musical heritage. Look for paintings, prints, or sculptures that depict famous composers, iconic musical venues, or musical motifs. These artistic pieces serve as visual reminders of the melodic ambiance that permeates Salzburg's streets and concert halls.

6. Music Festivals and Event Tickets:
   Immerse yourself in the live music experience by acquiring tickets to Salzburg's renowned music festivals and events. From the Salzburg Festival, featuring world-class performances in opera, theater, and orchestral music, to smaller chamber music concerts and recitals, there is a rich array of events to choose from. Enjoy the thrill of live performances and create lasting memories of Salzburg's musical prowess.

Salzburg's musical souvenirs provide a harmonious connection to the city's musical legacy and serve as cherished reminders of the melodic enchantment experienced during your visit. Whether you choose Mozart memorabilia, classical music recordings, musical instruments, or artistic pieces, these gifts celebrate the power of music and the rich cultural heritage of Salzburg. Indulge your passion for melody and take a piece of Salzburg's musical magic home with you.

IV

Part Four

Exploring Salzburg's Surroundings

Chapter 8

Day Trips from Salzburg : Natural Beauty and Cultural Excursions

Salzkammergut Region: Lakes, Mountains, and Alpine Serenity

Escape the bustling city and venture into the breath-taking Salzkammergut region, where pristine lakes, majestic mountains, and serene alpine landscapes await. Embark on a day trip from Salzburg and immerse yourself in the natural beauty and cultural treasures of this picturesque region.

1. Wolfgangsee: A Tranquil Alpine Retreat

Journey to the idyllic Wolfgangsee, a crystal-clear lake nestled amidst lush greenery and towering mountains. Take a leisurely stroll along the lakeside promenade, soaking in the tranquil atmosphere and picturesque views. Engage in water activities such as swimming, boating, or paddleboarding, or simply relax on the lakeshore and enjoy the serenity of this alpine oasis.

2. Hallstatt: A Fairytale Village

Step into the enchanting village of Hallstatt, known for its postcard-perfect beauty and rich history. Explore the charming streets lined with pastel-colored houses and flower-filled balconies. Visit the Hallstatt Salt Mine, where you can learn about the region's salt mining heritage and descend into the depths of the earth on an exciting underground tour. Capture breathtaking views of the village and the Hallstättersee from the Skywalk viewing platform.

3. Fuschlsee: Scenic Splendor and Outdoor Adventure

Discover the scenic splendor of Fuschlsee, a picturesque lake surrounded by rolling hills and dense forests. Take a leisurely hike along the lakeshore, breathing in the fresh alpine air and immersing yourself in the pristine natural surroundings. Enjoy water sports like kayaking or stand-up paddleboarding, or simply find a peaceful spot to relax and absorb the beauty of this hidden gem.

4. St. Gilgen and St. Wolfgang: Alpine Towns of Charm

Visit the neighboring alpine towns of St. Gilgen and St. Wolfgang, nestled on the shores of Wolfgangsee. Wander through the cobblestone streets, lined with charming shops, cafes, and traditional houses. Visit the birthplace of Mozart's mother in St. Gilgen or take a ride on the nostalgic Schafbergbahn cogwheel railway in St. Wolfgang, offering panoramic views of the surrounding mountains.

5. Gosau Valley: Alpine Splendor and Outdoor Pursuits

Embark on a journey to the breathtaking Gosau Valley, surrounded by towering peaks and lush meadows. Take in the awe-inspiring beauty of the Dachstein Glacier, which looms over the valley, and explore the pristine landscapes on hiking or biking trails. In winter, indulge in skiing or snowboarding on the slopes of the Gosau ski area, or simply marvel at the winter wonderland scenery.

6. Mondsee: Tranquil Lakeside Retreat

Discover the serene beauty of Mondsee, a charming town located on the shores of Lake Mondsee. Visit the iconic Mondsee Abbey, famous for its appearance in the wedding scene of "The Sound of Music." Explore the town's quaint streets, browse local boutiques, and enjoy a lakeside picnic surrounded by nature's tranquility.

The Salzkammergut region offers a captivating blend of natural beauty, alpine serenity, and cultural treasures, just a short distance from Salzburg. Embark on a day trip and immerse yourself in the picturesque landscapes, explore charming alpine towns, and bask in the tranquility of crystal-clear lakes. Experience the allure of this region and create lasting memories of its breathtaking scenery and cultural richness.

Berchtesgaden and Eagle's Nest: A Journey to History and Scenic Wonders

Embark on a captivating journey to Berchtesgaden and Eagle's Nest, where history, stunning landscapes, and remarkable architectural wonders come together. Explore the natural beauty of the Bavarian Alps, delve into the historical significance of the region, and be enchanted by the breathtaking views that await you.

1. Berchtesgaden Township: Alpine Charm and Rich History
   Begin your day trip in the charming township of Berchtesgaden, nestled amidst the majestic Bavarian Alps. Take a leisurely stroll through the picturesque streets, lined with traditional Bavarian houses, quaint shops, and cozy cafes. Learn about the town's intriguing history, from its salt mining heritage to its role as a former retreat for German royalty.

2. Obersalzberg: Historical Legacy and Documentation Center
   Venture to Obersalzberg, an area with a significant historical legacy. Explore the Documentation Center, which sheds light on the dark history of the Nazi regime and its connection to the area. Gain insights into the Third Reich's presence in the region and the impact it had on Berchtesgaden. Reflect on the historical significance and the lessons learned from this tumultuous era.

3. Eagle's Nest (Kehlsteinhaus): A Breathtaking Alpine Retreat
   Ascend to the Eagle's Nest, perched high on the summit of Kehlstein Mountain. Marvel at the engineering marvels that allowed Hitler's former mountain retreat to be built amidst the rugged Alpine landscape. As you reach the summit by special

bus, savor the panoramic views of the surrounding mountains and valleys. Step into the Eagle's Nest itself, where you can explore the historical exhibits and soak in the awe-inspiring vistas.

4. Königssee: Serene Beauty and Echoes of Nature

Experience the serene beauty of Königssee, a pristine lake surrounded by steep cliffs and emerald forests. Embark on a boat excursion that glides across the crystal-clear waters, offering breathtaking views of the surrounding landscape. Listen in awe as the famous "Echo of Königssee" reverberates through the mountains, a magical moment that adds to the allure of this natural wonder.

5. St. Bartholomew's Church: A Picturesque Landmark

Visit the iconic St. Bartholomew's Church, located on the shores of Königssee. Marvel at the striking red onion domes and the picturesque setting against the backdrop of towering mountains. Explore the interior of the church, which dates back to the 12th century, and admire the intricate details of the architecture and religious artifacts.

6. Almbach Gorge: Nature's Sculpted Masterpiece

Conclude your day trip with a visit to Almbach Gorge, a natural wonder that showcases the power of water and time. Walk along the well-maintained paths that wind through the gorge, marveling at the sculpted rock formations and the cascading waterfalls. Feel the refreshing mist on your face as you immerse yourself in this awe-inspiring display of nature's artistic prowess.

Berchtesgaden and Eagle's Nest offer a captivating blend of history, natural beauty, and architectural marvels. Immerse yourself in the rich historical legacy of the region, soak in the stunning alpine landscapes, and be amazed by the breathtaking views from Eagle's Nest. Experience the allure of Berchtesgaden and create lasting memories of this remarkable day trip.

Hallein Salt Mine: Delving into Subterranean Mysteries

Embark on an underground adventure as you journey to the Hallein Salt Mine, a fascinating destination that takes you back in time to the ancient world of salt mining. Delve into the subterranean mysteries of this historical site and discover the secrets hidden deep beneath the surface.

1. History of Salt Mining in Hallein:

Learn about the rich history of salt mining in Hallein, which dates back over 7,000 years. Explore the exhibits and displays that trace the evolution of salt extraction techniques throughout the centuries. Gain insights into the importance of salt as a valuable commodity, known as "white gold," and its impact on the region's economy and cultural heritage.

2. Mine Train Ride:

Embark on a thrilling mine train ride that takes you deep into the heart of the salt mine. Experience the excitement as you descend into the underground labyrinth, following in the footsteps of ancient miners. Feel the cool breeze and hear the rumble of the tracks as you journey through narrow tunnels and caverns, immersing yourself in the unique atmosphere of the mine.

3. Salt Slides and Underground Lake:

Engage in some fun and adventure as you slide down the salt slides, a unique feature of the Hallein Salt Mine. Feel the rush of adrenaline as you glide along the polished salt surfaces, experiencing the exhilaration that miners once felt during their breaks from work. Marvel at the underground lake, a hidden gem that reflects the ethereal beauty of its surroundings.

4. Multimedia Presentations:

Immerse yourself in multimedia presentations that bring the history and workings of the salt mine to life. Learn about the processes involved in salt extraction, from drilling and blasting to the transportation of salt. Gain a deeper understanding of the challenges faced by miners and the techniques they employed to extract this precious resource.

5. Salt Chamber and Salt Workshop:

Explore the intricately carved salt chamber, where you can witness the impressive craftsmanship of the miners. Admire the salt sculptures and learn about the artistic traditions associated with salt mining. Engage in a salt workshop, where you can create your own salt products or participate in interactive demonstrations that showcase the versatility of this mineral.

6. Salt Mine Museum and Shop:

Conclude your journey through the Hallein Salt Mine with a visit to the museum and shop. Discover artifacts, historical documents, and exhibits that offer further insights into the fascinating world of salt mining. Browse through the shop, where you can find unique salt-related products, including gourmet salts, spa products, and souvenirs to commemorate your underground adventure.

The Hallein Salt Mine offers a captivating glimpse into the subterranean world of salt mining. Delve into the mysteries of the underground, ride the mine train, slide down salt slides, and witness the artistic wonders created by the miners. Explore the history, engage in interactive experiences, and create lasting memories as you uncover the secrets of the Hallein Salt Mine.

Conclusion

Memories of Salzburg :

A s your time in Salzburg comes to a close, take a moment to reflect on the cherished memories you've created during your journey. Whether it was exploring the historic landmarks, immersing yourself in the city's musical heritage, indulging in culinary delights, or venturing into the natural wonders of the surrounding region, Salzburg has left an indelible mark on your heart.

Reflections on Cultural Immersion:
Consider the ways in which Salzburg's rich culture and heritage have influenced your own perspective. Reflect on the interactions with locals, the immersion in musical performances, the appreciation for traditional crafts, and the exploration of the city's history. These experiences have not only deepened your understanding of Salzburg but also broadened your horizons and enriched your own cultural journey.

Gratitude for the Journey:
Express gratitude for the opportunity to have embarked on

this travel adventure. Give thanks for the remarkable sights, the welcoming people, and the unforgettable experiences that have made your time in Salzburg truly special. Let the memories of this journey serve as a reminder of the beauty and wonders that exist in the world, and the transformative power of travel.

Carrying Salzburg with You:

As you bid farewell to Salzburg, know that the spirit of the city will always stay with you. Carry the melodies of Mozart, the charm of the historic center, the flavors of traditional Austrian cuisine, and the serenity of the alpine landscapes in your heart. Let these memories inspire you to seek new adventures, embrace new cultures, and continue to explore the world with a sense of wonder and curiosity.

Until We Meet Again:

Although your time in Salzburg may be coming to an end, know that the city will always be here, ready to welcome you back with open arms. Whether it's for another visit to relive the magic or to explore new hidden gems, Salzburg will be eagerly awaiting your return. Until we meet again, may your memories of Salzburg be a source of joy and inspiration.

As you bid farewell to Salzburg, take a moment to reflect on the transformative journey you've embarked on. Treasure the memories, embrace the cultural immersion, express gratitude for the experience, and carry the spirit of Salzburg with you wherever you go. Farewell for now, and may your future travels be filled with countless more extraordinary moments.

* * *

Appendix

- Language Primer: Useful German Phrases for Travelers

When traveling to Salzburg, having a few basic German phrases at your disposal can greatly enhance your experience. Here are some useful phrases to help you navigate the city and engage with locals:

1. Greetings and Basic Phrases:
  - Hello: Hallo
  - Good morning: Guten Morgen
  - Good afternoon: Guten Tag
  - Good evening: Guten Abend
  - Goodbye: Auf Wiedersehen
  - Please: Bitte
  - Thank you: Danke
  - Yes: Ja
  - No: Nein
  - Excuse me: Entschuldigung
  - I'm sorry: Es tut mir leid

2. Getting Around:
  - Where is...?: Wo ist...?
  - How much does it cost?: Wie viel kostet das?
  - I would like...: Ich möchte...
  - Can you help me?: Können Sie mir helfen?

- Where is the nearest...?: Wo ist der nächste...?

3. Dining and Ordering:

- I would like a table for two, please: Ich hätte gerne einen Tisch für zwei Personen, bitte.
- What do you recommend?: Was empfehlen Sie?
- The bill, please: Die Rechnung, bitte.
- Cheers!: Prost!

4. Directions and Transportation:

- Where is the nearest bus/train station?: Wo ist die nächste Bushaltestelle/Bahnhof?
- Which platform is the train to...?: Auf welchem Gleis fährt der Zug nach...?
- Can you call a taxi for me, please?: Können Sie mir bitte ein Taxi rufen?
- How do I get to...?: Wie komme ich nach...?

5. Emergency Situations:

- Help!: Hilfe!
- I need a doctor: Ich brauche einen Arzt.
- Where is the nearest hospital?: Wo ist das nächste Krankenhaus?
- I lost my passport: Ich habe meinen Reisepass verloren.

Remember to always approach locals with politeness and a friendly demeanor, even if your German language skills are limited. Most people in Salzburg are accustomed to interacting with tourists and will appreciate your efforts to communicate in their language.

This language primer provides basic phrases and is not intended to be a comprehensive German language guide. Consider bringing a pocket-sized German phrasebook or using a translation app for more specific or complex situations.

Enjoy your time in Salzburg, and may these phrases help you navigate the city with ease and connect with the locals in a meaningful way!

Safe travels!!!!!!!!!!!!!

Printed in Great Britain
by Amazon